My Little Book of
Baby Animals

by Camilla de la Bédoyère

Sandy Creek
NEW YORK

An Imprint of Sterling Publishing
1166 Avenue of The Americas
New York, NY, 10036

ISBN 978-1-4351-6347-8

Manufactured in Guangdong, China
Lot #:
4 6 8 10 9 7 5 3 2 1
02/16

Words in **bold** are explained in the glossary on page 60.

Contents

Asian Elephant

There are two types of elephants, Asian and African. Baby elephants feed on their mothers' milk, drinking up to 20 pints every day.

« A newborn calf is about 3 feet high from the ground to its shoulder.

Elephants visit **waterholes** or rivers to cool down. They suck water into their trunks, and spray it over their bodies.

⌄ **A female elephant will have six or seven calves in her lifetime.**

» **Calves cannot use their trunks at first, and must learn this skill.**

African Lion

Most big cats live alone, but lions live in family groups called prides. Baby lions are called cubs.

« Cubs spend most of the day sleeping.

» Cubs love to play, and practice their hunting skills.

Female lions hunt for food and male lions protect their family from other animals. Only males have manes of long fur on their heads and necks.

>> Fathers often look after the cubs when the mothers are away.

Siberian Tiger

Siberian tigers are the world's largest cats, but newborn cubs weigh less than a pet cat.

« Tigers have stripes, which help them to hide in a dark forest.

» A mother tiger has up to six cubs at a time.

Tiger mothers teach their cubs how to find and hunt for prey. By the age of two or three years, young tigers are fearless hunters.

>> Siberian tigers have thick fur because it often snows in their forest home.

9

Leopard

Leopard cubs copy their mothers to learn how to find food and climb. They will grow into incredible hunters.

« Leopards have a very good sense of smell.

Leopards live in forests, **grasslands**, mountains, and dry places. They can swim and often hide their food in trees.

>> Newborn cubs are gray with blue eyes, but they grow to look more like their parents.

<< The mother looks after her cubs until they are about two years old.

Cheetah

Cheetahs are the fastest of all big cats. The cub's mother catches food for it to eat.

>> **Cubs have blue-gray fur at first, but it soon turns yellow and spotty.**

Most cheetahs live in the African grasslands.
The cub's spots help it to hide in the grass.

>> Cheetahs have
long legs for fast
running.

ʌ Cheetah cubs
are born blind
and helpless.

Giraffe

Giraffe babies are called calves. Newborn calves stand up and walk just a few hours after being born.

A mother keeps her baby away from other giraffes for the first few weeks of its life.

« A newborn is about as tall as a man, but its mother is twice as tall.

⌄ A giraffe needs
a long neck to
reach the leaves
of tall trees.

^ The little
horns on a
giraffe's head
are called
ossicones.

(15)

Orangutan

The name orangutan means forest person, and these fruit-eating apes do look like people!

>> Orangutans kiss and wrap their arms around each other.

<< Orangutans like to sleep after they have feasted on fruit.

Baby orangutans stay with their mothers until they are about eight years old. They live in the **rainforests** of Borneo and Sumatra.

>> **Young orangutans can climb, swing, and leap.**

Mountain Gorilla

There are less than 800 mountain gorillas alive today. These great apes live in the cool, damp forests of Central Africa.

⩔ **Young gorillas love to play and cuddle.**

The father of the family is big and strong. He is called a silverback because his fur turns white as he gets older.

>> **Mountain gorillas eat plants.**

<< **When they are babies they stay with their mother all the time, often riding on her back or belly.**

Marmoset

Marmosets are little monkeys that live in the hot rainforests of South America. They chew holes in **gum trees** so they can eat the sticky gum that comes out.

« Most mothers have twins—two babies at a time.

Marmosets have long tails and some of them are very colorful. Baby marmosets cling to the adults' long fur as they leap through the trees.

« They quickly scamper through the trees, looking for insects and fruit to eat.

» Marmosets live together as families, and often share the job of caring for the babies.

Meerkat

Meerkats are a type of **mongoose**. They live in big family groups on the dry African grasslands.

Meerkats live in Africa where the weather can be very hot. Meerkats escape the heat by resting in their **burrows** and tunnels. This is also where the babies are born.

⌃ Both parents take care of the young.

« Little meerkats soon learn to stand up and look for danger.

« Other members of the pack babysit so the mother can search for food.

Prairie Dog

Prairie dogs live in grassy places and dig large burrows. Families all live together.

<< Prairie dog babies are called pups.

Prairie dogs are also called ground squirrels. When they are scared they jump, fluff up their fur, and call "yip".

≪ **Pups stay close to the burrow.**

⌄ **Members of the family greet each other with a kiss.**

Wild Boar

Wild boars are members of the pig family. Babies are born in spring and they are called piglets.

Wild boar families roam through forests and grassland, often living together in large groups called sounders.

>> **Young pigs have cream and brown stripes on their fur.**

« Most mothers
have between
four and six
babies at a
time.

» Piglets are born
in a nest that their
mother has made
from grass and
leaves.

Koala

A mother koala has a **pouch**, where she keeps her baby for the first six months of its life. Koalas live in **eucalyptus** forests in Australia.

« A baby stays with its mother until it is about one year old.

Older koala babies cling to their mother's back, or belly, when she climbs trees.

« They have sharp claws for gripping onto trees.

» Koalas spend most of their time in trees, asleep, or eating leaves.

29

Red Kangaroo

Kangaroos are **marsupials**. The mother has a pouch on her front for the baby. When the tiny baby, called a joey, is born, it must climb up its mother's belly to reach her pouch.

« Red kangaroos live in hot, dry places. They eat grass and leaves.

A newborn joey is tiny, but it grows quickly by feeding on its mother's milk. It stays in the pouch until it is about 190 days old.

∧ A joey is safe inside its mother's pouch.

∧ Kangaroos have long legs for leaping and kicking.

Common Porcupine

Baby porcupines have soft coats, but their parents are covered in sharp spines called quills.

<< Baby porcupines stay with their mother until they are two months old.

>> Porcupines climb trees to find berries, flowers, and fruit to eat.

Adult porcupines use their spines to defend themselves from other animals. They can also make their teeth chatter, and create bad smells.

⌃ **There are about 30,000 quills on a porcupine's body.**

Mountain Hare

Hares belong to the same family as rabbits.
Baby hares are called leverets.
Hares need long, strong legs
to run from danger.

« Their summer fur can look blue-brown,
so they are also called blue hares.

Mountain hares live in cold places where it snows in winter. Their fur turns white so they can hide from other animals.

« A leveret's big ears help it listen for danger.

« They leave their mothers when they are just three weeks old.

Virginia Opossum

A mother Virginia opossum can look after as many as 13 babies at a time. The tiny babies grow inside their mother's pouch, where they stay for about two months.

⌃ They have long, hairless tails that they use to hang from branches.

>> They climb trees and build dens inside tree holes, where they sleep.

Virginia opossums usually sleep in the day, and come out at night to find food to eat.

« Baby opossums ride on their mother's back.

Golden Hamster

Hamsters are popular pets all over the world. The golden hamster lives in the grasslands of Syria and Turkey.

>> Hamsters feed on flowers, seeds, nuts, and bugs.

<< Babies are born in the burrow, where they are safe and warm.

During the cold winters, hamsters spend much of their time sleeping in burrows, where they keep a **store** of food.

⌃ **The mother's cheeks are full of food for her babies.**

Gray Wolf

Wolf cubs live in big groups called packs. One mother and one father rule the pack, and they are called the **alpha** pair.

« Cubs are born in the spring, when it's not so cold and there is plenty of food.

» While the adult wolves hunt, the cubs can play.

Only the alpha pair has cubs, but the other wolves in the pack help to take care of the young wolves.

⚹ A gray wolf's fur can be gray, brown-red, or white.

Giant Panda

Giant pandas are rare bears that live in the **bamboo** forests of China. Newborn cubs are tiny, blind, and helpless.

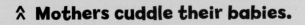
⌃ **Mothers cuddle their babies.**

Baby pandas open their eyes at three weeks of age and cannot move around on their own until they are about four months old.

« Most panda mothers have just one cub to look after.

∧ Young cubs like to climb trees.

Grizzly Bear

Grizzlies are a type of brown bear. They have enormous paws with long, sharp claws, which are used to dig for food and to fight.

« Adult grizzlies stay on the ground, but cubs love to climb trees.

Grizzlies often live near rivers so they can swim, play, and catch fish.

∧ Mother bears take care of their cubs until they are about two years old.

« A mother bear usually has two cubs at a time.

Canada Goose

Baby geese are called goslings. Adult Canada geese are brownish-gray, but their goslings are fluffy and yellow-gray.

« The goslings can fly when they are about ten weeks old.

∧ Canada geese eat grass that grows near a river, lake, or pond.

Mother geese lay their eggs in a nest
and keep them warm by lying on them.

^ Goslings follow
their mother
wherever she goes.

Flamingo

Flamingos are tall, elegant birds with long, slender legs. A flamingo egg is about the size of a grapefruit.

<< **Flamingo chicks stay together in a group called a creche.**

When they hatch, the chicks are covered with thick, gray **down**. They eat pink shrimp which makes their feathers turn pink as they get older.

>> A flamingo has wide, **webbed** feet for walking on mud.

⌃ Flamingos live by rivers and lakes in warm countries.

King Penguin

Penguins are black and white, but most penguin chicks look very different from their parents. King penguin chicks are covered in a coat of brown, fluffy feathers.

>> **Penguins cannot fly. They use their wings for swimming when they are fully grown.**

<< **A big group of penguins is called a colony.**

It is extremely cold in Antarctica, where king penguins live. They hunt for fish in the chilly ocean waters.

>> **Adult penguins bring food back to their chicks.**

Harp Seal

Harp seals are mammals that feed their young with milk. Seals live in water, but come to land to give birth to their pups.

ʌ **Pups have fluffy white fur, but adults have silvery smooth fur.**

Harp seal pups need their fluffy white fur to survive in the freezing ice and snow of the **Arctic**.

>> **Pups are born on ice, during February or March.**

<< **Seal pups cannot swim.**

Polar Bear

Polar bears live in and around the Arctic.
They are the biggest bears in the world.

^ **Most mothers have two
or three cubs to look after.**

Polar bear cubs are born in dens beneath layers of winter snow and emerge in the spring to look for food with their hungry mother.

∧ Their fur is yellow-white, but the skin underneath is black.

« Cubs have huge, wide paws for swimming and walking on slippery ice.

Snowy Owl

Snowy owls live in cold places around the **North Pole**, including Greenland, Canada, and Siberia. In the winter, they fly south to avoid the worst Arctic weather.

⋎ Snowy owls make a nest on the ground, and lay their eggs there.

⌃ Mothers protect their chicks, and fathers bring them food.

It can take both parents to feed all the chicks as there can be up to 16 owlets in one nest.

⌄ **Chicks are covered in soft feathers to keep them warm.**

Bottlenose Dolphin

Dolphins are ocean **mammals** and feed their young with milk. A baby dolphin is called a calf.

« Calves always swim very close to their mothers.

Dolphins are very smart animals. They are able to communicate with each other underwater. Dolphins mostly feed on fish and squid.

>> Dolphins come to the surface to breathe.

<< A dolphin's mouth is called a beak.

59

Glossary

alpha The most dominant leaders in a group.

arctic The icy and snowy northern part of planet Earth.

bamboo A type of grass that can grow as tall as a tree.

burrows Holes or tunnels that small animals dig and use as a home.

den An animal's home.

down Soft fine feathers which cover baby birds and grow under the feathers of adult birds.

eucalyptus A type of tree that grows mainly in Australia.

grasslands Large areas of land where the main plants that grow are grasses.

gum tree A type of tree that makes sticky gum in its bark.

mammals Warm-blooded animals, often with fur or hair, that feed their young with milk.

marsupials Animals that give birth to tiny babies, which feed and grow in their mother's pouch.

mongoose A small meat-eating mammal with a long body and a tail.

north pole The place at the top of the world.

pouch A pocket of skin on the stomach of some female animals, used to carry babies.

rainforest A warm forest where it rains every day.

store To put food in a safe place until it is needed.

waterhole A pool or pond where wild animals gather to drink.

webbed Toes which are connected by a layer of skin. Usually found on animals that live near water.

Index

Picture credits

(t=top, b=bottom, l=left, r=right, c=center)

All images are courtesy of FLPA Images except for pages 14 (l) © Tolf Kopfle / ardea.com, page 8 (l) Jean Michel Labat / aredea.com, page 9 (b) David J. Green - animals / Alamy. All images are courtesy of FLPA Images except for pages 14 (l) © Tolf Kopfle / ardea.com, page 8 (l) Jean Michel Labat / aredea. com, page 9 (b) David J. Green - animals / Alamy. All images are courtesy of FLPA Images except for pages 14 (l) © Tolf Kopfle / ardea.com, page 8 (l) Jean Michel Labat / aredea.com, page 9 (b) David J. Green - animals / Alamy. All images are courtesy of FLPA Images except for pages 14 (l) © Tolf Kopfle / ardea.com, page 8 (l) Jean Michel Labat / aredea.com, page 9 (b) David J. Green - animals / Alamy. All images are courtesy of FLPA Images except for pages 14 (l) © Tolf Kopfle / ardea.com, page 8 (l) Jean Michel Labat / aredea.com, page 9 (b) David J. Green - animals / Alamy. All images are courtesy of FLPA Images except for pages 14 (l) © Tolf Kopfle / ardea.com, page 8 (l) Jean Michel Labat / aredea. com, page 9 (b) David J. Green - animals / Alamy. All images are courtesy of FLPA Images except for pages 14 (l) © Tolf Kopfle / ardea.com, page 8 (l) Jean Michel Labat / aredea.com, page 9 (b) David J. Green - animals / Alamy. All images are courtesy of FLPA Images except for pages 14 (l) © Tolf Kopfle / ardea.com, page 8 (l) Jean Michel Labat / aredea.com, page 9 (b) David J. Green - animals / Alamy. All images are courtesy of FLPA Images except for pages 14 (l) © Tolf Kopfle / ardea.com, page 8 (l) Jean Michel Labat / aredea.com, page 9 (b) David J. Green - animals / Alamy. All images are courtesy of FLPA Images except for pages 14 (l) © Tolf Kopfle / ardea.com, page 8 (l) Jean Michel Labat / aredea.com, page 9 (b) David J. Green - animals / Alamy. All images are courtesy of FLPA Images except for pages 14 (l) © Tolf Kopfle / ardea.com, page 8 (l) Jean Michel Labat / aredea.com, page 9 (b) David J. Green - animals / Alamy.